THE LEBANESE IN AMERICA

L THE EBANESE
IN AMERICA

Elsa Marston Harik

Lerner Publication Company · Minneapolis

Front cover: *The Abraham department store in Canadian, Texas, was one of the many small retail businesses established by immigrants from Lebanon.* Page 2: *Solomon Casseb (right) was the first of his family to emigrate from Lebanon, arriving in Texas in 1901 at the age of 16. He was later joined by his widowed mother, Annie Swia Casseb (center), and his younger brother, George (left).*

For Muna Harik

Library of Congress Cataloging-in-Publication Data

Marston, Elsa.
   The Lebanese in America.

   (The In America series)
   Includes index.
   Summary: A survey of Lebanese immigration to the
United States with a discussion of the contributions
made by Lebanese to various areas of American life.
   1. Lebanese Americans—Juvenile literature.
[1. Lebanese Americans] I. Title. II. Series.
E184.L34M37   1987   973'.049275692   86-34407
ISBN 0-8225-0234-8 (lib. bdg.)
ISBN 0-8225-1032-4 (pbk.)

Manufactured in the United States of America

1 2 3 4 5 6 7 8 9 10 97 96 95 94 93 92 91 90 89 88 87

CONTENTS

1
THE LAND THEY CAME FROM

Traditional Arabic patterns in mosaic and stone decorate this room in the 19th-century palace of Beit-ed-Din, located on the slopes of Mount Lebanon.

On the eastern shore of the Mediterranean Sea rises a high mountain range, located between Israel on the south and Syria on the north and east. For thousands of years, this range, traditionally called Mount Lebanon, has given an identity to the tiny country we know today as Lebanon.

Since Biblical times, the mountains of Lebanon have been famous for their beauty. Snow covers the high peaks for most of the year, while the lower slopes are green with pines and fruit trees. Majestic cedars, tall and spreading, once grew abundantly in the mountains but are now found in only a few spots. The most famous is a grove high in the northern part of the range, today known simply as The Cedars. Long considered a symbol of the beauty and endurance of Lebanon, the cedar's image appears on the flag of the modern nation.

The famous Cedars of Lebanon wear a heavy coat of snow during the winter months.

This small country, about the size of the state of Connecticut, has a great variety of terrain packed within its narrow borders. To the east of Mount Lebanon lies a flat valley called the Beka'a. Today as in the past, the fertile land of the valley provides much of the wheat, vegetables, and grapes that makes Lebanese food world-famous. On the far side of the Beka'a rises a mountain range that runs parallel to Mount Lebanon. Known appropriately as the Anti-Lebanon, this arid range forms part of the country's eastern border with Syria.

Although the Anti-Lebanon range is dry and barren, most of Lebanon is blessed with an abundant supply of water. Rain and snow fall from October to May, feeding the springs that are found everywhere in the country, some mere trickles and others great torrents of water.

Just as important in Lebanon's history as the life-giving springs is the sea, which lies on the western border of this 31-mile-wide country. Since earliest times, the sea has been a highway that has connected Lebanon to the rest of the world. The country's location on the easternmost edge of the Mediterranean and the westernmost corner of Asia has made it both a crossroads of traffic and trade and a tempting prize for nations seeking conquest.

Ancient Lebanon

In ancient times, the region that would become Lebanon was inhabited by people known as Phoenicians. The Phoenicians came into the area from the south around 3,000 B.C., and by 1,000 B.C., they had established themselves as the outstanding traders of the ancient world. The pharoahs of Egypt were among the Phoenicians' best customers, purchasing timber cut from the tall cedars of Mount Lebanon.

The Phoenicians were known for their skill not only as traders but also as navigators. From cities like Tyre, Sidon, and Byblos, their ships set sail for all parts of the Mediterranean. Using their knowledge of navigation by the stars, Phoenician sailors even made their way into the Atlantic, reaching Britain in the north and sailing south around Africa. In their travels, the Phoenicians took with them their alphabet, made up of symbols standing for sounds that could be combined into words. The Phoenician alphabet eventually became the source of the Greek and Roman alphabets and those of most modern Western languages.

Phoenician influence declined around 800 B.C., and over the next centuries, the great coastal cities were controlled by other powers: Assyrian, Babylonian, Persian, and Greek. Greek rule began when Alexander the Great captured the city of Tyre in 332 B.C. The Greek influence lasted about 300 years and left a deep mark on Lebanon. Then, around 63 B.C., the Romans appeared on the eastern shores of the Mediterranean.

The ruins of the Phoenician port of Byblos, one of the oldest known human settlements in the world. Founded around 5000 B.C., Byblos was an important center of Phoenician commerce. Among the trade goods that passed through the port was papyrus, a form of paper used in many parts of the ancient world. The Greeks adapted the name Byblos *to mean "paper" and later "book." From this usage eventually came the English word* Bible.

The 600 years of Roman rule were probably the most peaceful and prosperous in Lebanon's history. The population grew rapidly, and good roads united the country, which had become a part of the Roman province of Syria. In the valley of Beka'a, a magnificent new city called Heliopolis was erected. (The ruined temples of the city, now known as Baalbek, still stand in the fertile valley.) Ancient Tyre became an important Roman city, and its splendid temples and huge race track gave evidence of the Romans' love of pomp and excitement. At Berytus (Beirut), a law school second only to those in Rome attracted students from many parts of the Roman Empire.

In 554 A.D., Berytus was destroyed by an earthquake that marked the final stage of the Roman period in Lebanon. The next wave of conquerors came from the south, from Arabia. Inspired by the newly established religion of Islam, the Arabs swept through many of the Middle Eastern countries in the early 600s. Most of the people of Lebanon had been converted to Christianity during the years of Roman rule. Exhausted by warfare and a long period of decline, however, many of them welcomed the conquerors and the religion they brought.

One group of Lebanese Christians, called Maronites after a religious leader, did not accept the change but chose to isolate themselves in the northern part of Mount Lebanon. The rest of Lebanon became an Arabized and largely Muslim country like its neighbors.

Above: *The temples of Bacchus and Jupiter dominate the ruins of Baalbek, known to the Romans as Heliopolis, the city of the sun.* Below: *The Sea Castle was built by Crusaders in 1227 A.D. to protect the harbor of the ancient city of Sidon. The Arabic script on the boat in the foreground represents another of the important world cultures that have shaped the history of Lebanon.*

New Rulers, New Conflicts

Around the year 1100, a new group of invaders came to the eastern Mediterranean world. They were Crusaders from Europe who were determined to win the holy places of Christianity away from Muslim control. In the process, they also hoped to acquire some of the fabulous riches of the East.

The Crusaders established themselves in Lebanon and built massive castles, towers, and churches, many of which can be seen today. Muslim forces resisted this invasion of their territory, and within 200 years, the Crusaders' dream of creating Middle Eastern kingdoms was over. One lasting effect of this East-West contact, however, was a link between the Maronites, who had supported the Crusades, and France, the European country from which many of the Crusading knights came.

After the Crusaders left, Lebanon was controlled by the Mameluke rulers of Egypt for about 200 years. This was a period of oppression, economic decline, and natural disasters. Next came powerful invaders from the north. When the Ottoman Turks spread over the Middle East, conquering Lebanon and the surrounding countries in 1516, they established a rule that would last 400 years. These, too, were years of stagnation—except in Mount Lebanon.

The people of the mountain, Christians and Muslims of minority sects, had long experience in running their own

Osman I was the first sultan of the Ottoman Empire, a powerful state that controlled Lebanon for many centuries.

affairs. Their system of government, ruled by a prince and local feudal lords, worked fairly well, and their strongholds in the rugged mountains were not easy for outsiders to control. For these reasons, the Ottoman rulers allowed a large measure of self-rule to the people of Mount Lebanon. On the other hand, the cities along the coast and the territory east of the mountains were under direct Turkish control.

In the 1600s, a leader from Mount Lebanon named Fakhr-ed-Deen II succeeded in uniting much of Lebanon. An

11

Ameer Basheer Shihab governed Mount Lebanon from a splendid palace located in the mountain town of Beit-ed-Din. In the 20th century, the palace was used as a summer residence by the presidents of Lebanon.

enlightened ruler, he strengthened the country by building roads, improving agriculture, and promoting trade with Europe. The Lebanese people prospered. Eventually, however, the Ottomans decided that they could no longer allow so much independence in Mount Lebanon. Fakhr-ed-Deen was captured and executed in 1635. Today he is still regarded as a great Lebanese hero.

About 150 years after the death of Fakhr-ed-Deen, a second strong leader emerged in Mount Lebanon. Basheer Shihab was *ameer* (prince) of the mountain for most of the years from 1783 to 1840. A tough ruler, he was nonetheless fair and progressive. Under his leadership, there was more freedom, justice, and well-being in Mount Lebanon than anywhere else in the Middle East. Basheer's downfall came about when he lent his support to new rulers from Egypt, whose government was at first fair but then grew more oppressive. The people of Lebanon rose up. With the help of the combined forces of England, France, and Ottoman Turkey, they put an end to the alliance with Egypt in 1840.

During this period, the population of Mount Lebanon was changing, with Maronite Christians moving south into territories long held by the Druze, people belonging to a faith related to Islam. Tension grew among the different religious groups, and it was made worse by interference from outside powers. In 1860, open fighting and massacres broke out on the mountain, and the Christians got the worst of it. Following these dark days, the European countries persuaded the Ottomans to set up a new form of self-rule for Mount Lebanon. This system, which brought back peace and stability, lasted until the time of World War I.

Independence

The end of the war brought defeat to Ottoman Turkey, but Lebanon and the other Arab countries under Ottoman control were not given their freedom. Instead, England and France divided the territory between them for the purpose of preparing the countries for eventual independence. This arrangement was known as the Mandates.

Because of its long ties with France, going back to the time of the Crusades, Lebanon was put under the mandatory government of that European power. Previously considered a part of geographic Syria, Mount Lebanon was now

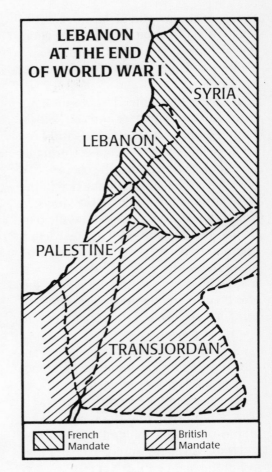

LEBANON AT THE END OF WORLD WAR I

SYRIA

LEBANON

PALESTINE

TRANSJORDAN

French Mandate   British Mandate

the central part of a separate state. In addition to the mountain, the new country included the coast, the Beka'a Valley, and part of the Anti-Lebanon mountains.

In 1943, after considerable nudging from Lebanese leaders and the British, France finally stepped aside, and Lebanon became a free republic. During its time under French rule, the country had absorbed much French influence in the form of language, education, and culture. The Maronite Christians in particular had been favored by the French and had taken a prominent role in the life of the country. After independence, leadership of the national government was divided among the several different religious groups, but the Maronites had the most power.

As a free country, Lebanon grew rapidly, developing in commerce and modernization. During the 1960s and early 1970s, the capital city of Beirut was a true boom town, and the country as a whole became a symbol of progress, freedom, business enterprise, and luxury in the Middle East. Yet tensions existed under Lebanon's material success. The different religious groups had opposing ideas about the country's policies toward the other Arab states and toward the superpowers of East and West. The balance of power also seemed to be shifting as the Muslims, increasing in population faster than the Christians, began to challenge the Maronites' strong role in government.

The first sign of trouble came in 1958 when armed conflict broke out between the government and groups of Muslim rebels. The conflict was resolved in a few months, and during the 1960s, more careful and progressive leaders ran the country. The underlying problems, however, did not go away. One major source of friction was the presence in Lebanon of about half a million Palestinian refugees who had been forced to leave their homes when the state of Israel was created in 1948. The military actions of the Palestinians led to Israeli attacks on their bases in Lebanon, and thus on Lebanese territory.

Since 1975, Lebanon has been torn by a many-sided conflict. The Muslims want a greater share in power and in the nation's economic well-being. The Christians, by and large, want to hold onto their rights and their privileged position; otherwise, many fear, they may lose everything. The Palestinians want to keep their bases on Lebanese soil. The Israelis want to put an end to attacks by the Palestinians and also to persuade Lebanon—by force, if necessary—to adopt a friendly position toward Israel. Neighboring Syria wants increased control over Lebanon's policies.

The Lebanese people in general want an end to the fighting that has cost almost 100,000 lives, mostly of civilians, and has destroyed large parts of Beirut and other communities. The nation's inhabitants have lived in fear and hardship for many long years. Yet the destructive fighting continues, and no solution to Lebanon's complex problems is yet in sight.

The People of Lebanon Today

For at least 1,500 years, Mount Lebanon was a sort of haven for religious sects that would not have been allowed to live in such freedom elsewhere. As a result, Lebanon has traditionally had a population made up of many different groups. Both in the present and the past, this varied population has greatly influenced Lebanese history.

Of the approximately 3 million people in Lebanon today (no precise figures are available), a little more than half are Muslim and the rest are Christian. The largest number of Lebanese Muslims are Shi'ites, followers of a branch of Islam that differs from the "mainstream" Sunni group on some points. The Shi'ites, on the whole, have long been the poorest and least educated group in Lebanon, many of them living in the less developed rural parts of the country, the south and the Beka'a. In very recent years, however, they have begun to play a much larger role in Lebanese life.

A smaller number of Lebanese Muslims are members of the Sunni sect. They are mostly city people and prominent in business and the professions. In some ways, the Sunni Muslims share power and interests with the Christians; in other ways, the two groups are rivals. A third religious sect is made up of the Druze, who follow a religion that originated from Islam. Traditionally, they are mountain people with strong loyalty

In January 1976, these buildings in Beirut were set ablaze by the rocket and mortar fire of groups fighting within the city. The destructive civil war still holds Lebanon in its grip.

15

The Great Mosque in Tripoli is a place of worship for the city's Muslim inhabitants. The minaret of the mosque was once the bell tower of a cathedral built by the Crusaders.

to their clan leaders and also a progressive attitude toward education and business enterprise.

The Christians of Lebanon belong to several groups that differ in their religious practices and in their position in Lebanese society. Some of these groups are what is known as Eastern Rite Catholics; they are part of the Roman Catholic Church, but they use ancient liturgies that differ from the religious rites of the Catholic Church as it exists in Europe and the United States. The Maronites belong in this category. A smaller Eastern Rite sect in Lebanon are the Melkites, sometimes called Greek Catholics.

Another major Christian group in Lebanon, second in size to the Maronites, is the Greek Orthodox Church, part of the ancient branch of Christianity that traces its origins back to the days of the Byzantine Empire. Greek Orthodox Christians use religious rituals similar to those of the Eastern Rite Catholics, but they do not accept the authority of the pope in Rome.

In addition to the Greek Orthodox, there is an Armenian Orthodox Church in Lebanon. Its members, who fled from Turkey early in the 20th century, have their own form of Christianity and their own language. Several other smaller Christian sects, including Protestant, also have followers.

On the whole, the Christians in Lebanon are leaders in education, business, and the professions. The Maronites, who held out for so long in the high mountains, still make up the country's largest and most powerful Christian sect. Many Maronites consider themselves the "most Lebanese" of the country's inhabitants. Members of the other Christian groups are generally more in tune with Arab culture and attitudes than are the Maronites. They more readily identify themselves as Arabs, whereas many Maronites feel distinctly and exclusively Lebanese.

The many different religious groups in Lebanon give their followers a strong sense of identity and security. But the division of the people into these groups can also encourage suspicion, rivalry, and conflict. On the other hand, it must be noted that more often in Lebanon's history than not, the religious groups have gotten along with little trouble.

Lebanon is a cosmopolitan country. The Lebanese in all their variety are joined by Armenians, Palestinians, and Arabs from other states who come for business or vacation. In normal times, many Europeans, Americans, and Asians also flock to Lebanon for business, travel, and education. It is truly a meeting place of East and West, blending the ideas and technology of the West with the traditional attitudes and customs of the Arab and Islamic world.

What seems to unite the inhabitants of Lebanon most successfully is the spirit of enterprise. People want to get ahead, to make the most of themselves. They want the best education and the best jobs. They succeed brilliantly in the professions, and, like the Phoenicians, they are energetic traders and business people. They love the comforts of the old country—the spectacular scenery, the delicious food—but beyond that, they yearn for the modern. New ideas and new ways to earn a living: the Lebanese are quick to grasp them all.

The slopes of Mount Lebanon, all but the steepest, are carved into innumerable little terraces where people once grew their basic food. These terraces are proof of the people's determination to survive and even prosper in a difficult environment. In the mid-19th century, many of those people were just waiting for a chance to show the world what more they could do with their energy and cleverness. As in the days of the Phoenicians, the Lebanese of this period were among the world's most enthusiastic emigrants, ready to start making a new history in a new place.

This silver coin from Sidon pictures one of the ships that carried Phoenician sailors to many parts of the ancient world. In the 19th century, the people of Lebanon once more set out on voyages to seek their fortunes in other lands.

2
WHY THEY LEFT HOME

A terraced hillside on Mount Lebanon

Hard Times on the Mountain

For many centuries, the Lebanese people chose to live high on the slopes of their beautiful mountains. What held them there was not the scenery but the safety provided by a terrain so rugged that few outsiders ventured very far into it.

Despite this protection, life in the mountains did have its drawbacks. The people had to depend on the land to support them, but the soil that could be farmed, while fertile, was very limited and full of rocks. At the same time, the homes were full of children, as the homes of peasant families usually are. During the 19th century, the population of the mountain also grew rapidly due to an earlier inflow of immigrants from Syria who had come to Mount Lebanon because of the greater freedom there.

But the land, no matter how skillfully carved into terraces, could feed only so many people.

Overcrowding was also caused by the fact that, after 1860, the special government for Mount Lebanon was limited to the mountain alone. The coastal plain with its ports and the Beka'a Valley was under direct Ottoman rule. Therefore the people of the mountain were more confined than they had been in the past.

Although the Lebanese were deeply attached to their native villages, by the 1870s, the need for more room was forcing many people to think about looking elsewhere. Migration had, in fact, been going on within the country for two or three generations. Many Christians of the northern mountains were moving south. As a result of this migration, Beirut grew from a town of about 5,000 at the start of the 1800s to a city of 120,000 by the century's end. The mountain people were not too firmly rooted to leave in search of a better life.

Several reasons besides overcrowding impelled them. For one thing, the economy of Lebanon was suffering. Aside from such crafts as weaving and pottery, there were few resources for industry on Mount Lebanon and no money for development. Trade was never easy over the chains of mountains that ran the length of the country.

The thriving silk industry, in which Lebanese villagers cultivated silkworms to produce raw silk for the textiles of Italy and France, began to decline after the opening of the Suez Canal in 1869.

Weaving was one of the traditional crafts practiced by the people of Mount Lebanon during the late 1800s.

With the Canal, European trade with East Asia increased rapidly. Lebanese silk, produced by old-fashioned methods, could not compete with that of Japan and China. On top of this, a widespread disease afflicted grapevines in the 1870s, ruining much of the wine production.

Meanwhile, most of the rulers of Mount Lebanon took little interest in building up the country. The common people were poor and getting poorer. Neither from the Ottoman overlords nor from the local ruling classes did they see signs of things getting better.

19

The Ottoman emperors ruled their vast domain from the palace of Topkapi (above and right) in Istanbul. They lived in great luxury, while many of their subjects were poor and oppressed.

Political problems, as well as economic stagnation, encouraged many people to look for greater freedom elsewhere. Even though conditions were fairly secure on the mountain after 1860, the hand of the Ottoman Empire could still be felt everywhere in the form of heavy taxes and restrictions, often arbitrary and unfair. The overall presence of the Ottomans, which had gone on for nearly four centuries, showed no tendency toward more progressive rule.

Military conscription was another problem. Muslims had always been subject to military draft, a dreaded fate, and after 1909, Christians living outside the boundaries of Mount Lebanon were also liable. Many men and boys fled the country to avoid being forced into the Turkish army.

Religion, too, had a bearing on some decisions to emigrate—though it should not be overemphasized. No religious strife flared openly in the decades between 1860 and World War I, but tensions persisted. Some Christians thought of finding a place to live where they would not feel at odds with both the foreign overlords and the great majority of the population.

In many cases, of course, personal problems drove people from home. A quarrel with a parent or cousin, conflict with neighbors, a disappointed love or broken engagement, or a disastrous harvest might make a young man decide to try his luck elsewhere. A father might send a troublesome son away, hoping a new life would encourage him to straighten up. Some young people simply longed to see the world. But for the most part, the main personal reason for emigration was the desire of the emigrants to make something of themselves.

New Lives in Other Lands

In the last decades of the 19th century, the whole world seemed to be opening up to Lebanese seeking new horizons. The United States, South America, Egypt, West Africa, Australia . . . all these places promised freedom and great possibilities. More and more young men began to contrast their villages, where they had little but family, fresh air, and scenery, with the great outside world, where they could work hard and earn big rewards.

Intellectuals and other educated persons were the first to leave Lebanon. They headed for Egypt, where educated men were needed to modernize the country's administration in the 1860s and 1870s. When the British took control of Egypt in 1882, the progressive atmosphere further encouraged intellectuals to leave Lebanon for Cairo. There they led the efforts responsible for renewed interest in Arabic literature and awareness of the Arab spirit. Lebanese traders and businessmen soon followed and became immensely prosperous.

It was the Americas, though, that promised the most for the most people. South American countries such as Brazil, Argentina, and Venezuela lured many Lebanese emigrants. But the United States, a land of stable government and religious freedom as well as seemingly unlimited wealth, offered the most glowing attractions.

The first Lebanese immigrants arrived in the United States in the late 1870s. Proof came quickly that these "pioneers" had made a good choice in emigrating to America. Though penniless when leaving their villages, they

The United States was a land of promise to Lebanese immigrants seeking better lives.

were soon sending money back home. Village people, who had supplied their own basic needs before this, became money-conscious almost overnight. Everyone wanted cash to satisfy new desires for luxuries and as a symbol of prestige. Some young men came home in person, and their clothes were ample evidence of their success. More sent enthusiastic letters. "Post offices," usually a centrally located shop such as the barber's, soon became the center of social activity. Everyone gathered here regularly to see who was receiving news and money from America.

American citizens, too, advertised their country in Lebanon. Missionaries, primarily Presbyterian, had been coming to Mount Lebanon and to Beirut and other coastal cities since 1819. They started many schools, including, in 1866, the Syrian Protestant College—later to become the famous American University of Beirut.

These American teachers did not try to induce the Lebanese to leave their country. Indirectly, however, they held out a very attractive picture of the United States by teaching English and other subjects such as American history and geography. Their own educated backgrounds, idealism, and democratic views also spoke well for the country they represented.

Many American tourists also visited Lebanon, the Holy Land, and Egypt in the 19th century. They needed the services of guides and interpreters, who learned about the United States from the visitors and in turn told their

The first graduating class of the Syrian Protestant College (later the American University of Beirut), 1870. These students learned a great deal about the United States from the teachers of the influential school.

relatives and friends about Americans and their country. News of the big international fairs in Chicago (1893) and in St. Louis (1904) also reached Mount Lebanon and turned more people's thoughts toward the United States.

Once enough people decided to leave home, emigration became more businesslike. Money-lenders appeared on the scene to provide the necessary funds. Steamship agents even toured the mountain villages to encourage people to buy tickets to the "land of opportunity." There was, however, no wholesale contracting of labor by American employers, like the exploitation that took place among poor Italian and Greek emigrants. The Lebanese went as individuals, on their own initiative or persuaded by relatives and friends. Their passage was merely made easier by the money-lenders and steamship services.

By the 1890s, the trickle of emigration to the United States from the mountains and plains of Lebanon had become a stream. After 1908, when Ottoman rule turned more harsh and Christians became subject to military conscription, the stream became a flood—a flood, that is, for a place as small as Lebanon. Accurate figures of early Lebanese immigrants to the United States are hard to determine, largely because of confusion in the record-keeping. The figures we have for the early 20th century, however, show an increase in Lebanese immigrants from 2,900 in 1900 to 6,300 in 1910. With war clouds looming over Europe and the Middle East, more than 9,000 immigrants came in both 1913 and 1914.

The people of Lebanon, though not engaged in combat, suffered terribly during the period of World War I. They were subjected to repressive measures by the Ottomans, blockade by the Allied powers, famine and disease epidemics, renewed religious tension, and even invasions of grasshoppers. A great many, possibly as many as one-fourth of the entire mountain population, died from starvation and sickness during these years.

Doubtless many people would have liked to leave the devastated land but were prevented by the hazards of sea travel during war and by the exhausting demands of their daily lives. Emigration to the United States dwindled to 210 in 1918. By 1922 it had jumped once more to 5,100.

Soon, though, the United States government, in a conservative and fearful reaction to world events, imposed severe restrictions on immigration from Lebanon and Syria. By 1925 the number of new arrivals from that part of the world had dropped to only 450, and by 1932 it was down to 284. For the next 20 years or so, few new immigrants came, and many of those that did were family members of persons already settled here.

From 1950 to the mid-1970s, some Lebanese people continued to emigrate to United States. They had different backgrounds from the emigrants of the past, however, and came for different purposes, primarily education and pro-

The bloody conflict in Lebanon during the mid-1970s brought a new wave of Lebanese immigrants to the United States.

fessional advancement. In 1975, a new wave of emigration from Lebanon began, set off by the civil and international conflict in the area, as a later chapter will explain.

The main reasons why the Lebanese left the majestic mountains that had sheltered them for so many centuries are not so very different from the factors that have impelled other people to emigrate. They left to escape overcrowding and poverty at home and to seek a better life, religious security, and personal freedom. The people who made the move overseas, however, differed in some important ways from those who did not feel the call to leave. Certain characteristics of these emigrants helped shape the course of their lives in the new country.

3
WHO WERE THE IMMIGRANTS?

Many students who passed through the main gate of the American University of Beirut eventually came to the United States as immigrants.

Those Who Came First

Influenced by American Protestant missionaries and eager to pursue religious studies, Antoun el-Bishalany arrived in Boston in 1854. Only two years later, aged 29, he was dead of tuberculosis. Though often mentioned as the first Lebanese to reach these shores with a dream of self-fulfillment, Bishalany was nevertheless the exception that often proves the rule. Most of those who followed him came not with the desire for learning, but with the single-minded goal of making money.

In 1876, when the International Exposition was held in Philadelphia, a few Lebanese and Syrian merchants came to sell curios from the Holy Land. These items were in great demand, and word soon reached Lebanon of the Americans' interest in such objects. Other merchants were quick to follow and also did well. Before long, people were leaving villages all over the mountain and the Beka'a Valley in search of the "gold" in the streets of America.

This drawing by Frank Leslie shows one of the popular bazaars at the International Exposition in Philadelphia, where merchants from Lebanon and other Middle Eastern countries sold exotic wares.

A few of the early comers were educated individuals with business experience. Most of the Lebanese "pioneers" in the United States, however, were young men with little or no schooling and no money behind them or even in their pockets. And virtually all were Christians from the several different sects found in Lebanon.

Reasons why Lebanese Christians were the first to emigrate to the Americas are not hard to find. The Maronites had long been in contact with the Christian West because of their relationship with the Roman Catholic Church and because of the work of French missionaries. When American Protestant missionaries came to Lebanon in the

19th century, they established schools offering modern learning in both Arabic and English to whoever would accept it. Increasing numbers of Christians, most from the Orthodox and Melkite sects, attended the American schools and the Syrian Protestant College (American University of Beirut).

Because of the missionaries and their schools, many Lebanese Christians had some acquaintance with the cultures of Europe and the United States. They had a natural feeling of sympathy with the Christian countries, even though they knew that the forms of Christianity in the West were different from the Eastern ones. America, they expected, would be a welcoming place for them, and they would feel at home.

Muslims, on the other hand, had a different reaction to the prospect of going to America. For one thing, their religious beliefs made them reluctant to accept the education and culture of the Christian countries. They did not turn their backs on emigration as such, for many, particularly Shi'ites, went to the predominantly Muslim countries of West Africa to work as traders. But Muslims were reluctant to go to the United States simply because it was a Christian country. They knew there would be no mosques in America and probably little understanding of or sympathy for their faith. They feared the prospect of losing their religion and, worse, of seeing their children grow up without Islam.

Yet by the early 20th century, more and more Muslims in Lebanon, includ-

ing some girls, were becoming educated along modern lines. They went to both Western mission schools and to schools run by a recently formed Islamic society, the Makassed. Gradually, a few Muslims became willing to face the unknown in return for the economic advantages offered by the United States.

As the international situation worsened in the early 1900s, Ottoman Turkey began to conscript Muslims into its armies with an even heavier hand, and flight to America became a more attractive prospect. By the outbreak of World War I, a few hundred young Muslims had emigrated to the United States, most of them after 1908. Even so, these Muslim "pioneers" were not typical of their people but, rather, ambitious and adventurous young men ready to break away from tradition.

Shortly after World War I, more Lebanese Muslims came to the United States. They tended to settle together and reinforce each other religiously. Dearborn and Detroit, Michigan, have both had sizeable Lebanese Muslim groups since the 1920s.

As for the Druze, some of them had shown interest in American education much earlier than had the Muslims, even sending their daughters to an American school for Druze girls started in 1834. Around the turn of the century, a number of young Druze men started crossing to the New World. Both adventurous and community-minded, a group of Druze formed a society in 1907 at a spot about as far from their homeland as possible—Seattle, Washington.

A mosque in Dearborn, Michigan. Muslim immigrants from Lebanon have made their homes in this American city since the 1920s.

Temporary Sojourn in America

Regardless of their religion, the intention of the first emigrants was to make a lot of money as fast as they could and then return home. In their native villages, they expected, they would then be admired and honored. They could marry good wives, build fine houses, help their families and villages, and spend the rest of their days in comfort, free of the threat of poverty. This was the common plan for both Christians and Muslims.

The early emigrants, in fact, *had* to "make good." Families typically combined all their possible resources to send a promising young man to America as an investment, and he was under pressure to live up to their expectations.

Because they regarded their stay in America as only temporary, the pioneers made no attempt to establish homes at first. Instead, they lived very simply, even roughly. For example, five to ten men or two families would crowd into a single bare room. They worked long, hard hours under difficult conditions and saved every penny they could. Rather than spend five cents on a trolley, they walked. They brewed their coffee in the common kitchen of the rundown house where they lived with several other Lebanese individuals and families, rather than "wasting" a few pennies at a coffee house.

The early immigrants made money—

quite a lot for those days—and saved most of it for the return trip to Lebanon. Some of their earnings were sent home to share the good fortune with relatives. The story is told of one young man from the village of Baskinta, high in the mountains, who arrived in New York City in 1888 in the midst of a blizzard. Undiscouraged, he set off to make his way as a trader, traveling through New York state and eventually getting as far west as Cheyenne, Wyoming. After three years, he sent $200 to his brother in Baskinta. As soon as word got around, 40 young men left the village to try their luck in America.

Staying On

A few of the early emigrants probably left Lebanon with no intention of returning. For some Christians, particularly those living outside Mount Lebanon, the primary reason for emigration may have been to escape the oppression of a foreign ruler and the uneasiness caused by religious differences. These people no doubt had long-range plans to stay in the United States.

But this was not true of the great majority of early emigrants. They do not seem to have viewed their departure from Lebanon as an escape from an intolerable situation, nor had anyone forced them to leave. They did not have bitter memories of the home country. They simply wanted a better chance, which would ensure a more comfortable life for them and their families

When Lebanese immigrants married, like this young couple in Utah, they were usually ready to make a permanent home in the United States.

when they returned home.

For most of the pioneers, however, the lure of the good life in America overcame these intentions. When they saw how much money they could earn, it was tempting to want more. When they settled down and established small stores and businesses, it was hard to abandon their stakes.

When they bought homes (and home ownership was always highly valued among the Lebanese), they became even more firmly rooted in this land.

Yet they were determined to leave their cherished homeland. The opportunities for personal and family welfare in the New World were powerful persuaders for emigration, at least on a temporary basis.

Popular poetry, which holds such an important place in Arabic hearts, reflects the mixed emotions of the early emigrants. Here are two contrasting songs from the early 1900s.

Lebanon, I'm saying goodbye with tears on my cheeks,
And I'm leaving my soul with you as a reminder of me.
I've not stopped hoping I'm returning to you,
And I'll celebrate at your springs two thousand evenings.

We climbed to the top of the boat and ascended,
And the eye of the mother went with us.
As for us, we'll never see our country again,
And in New York we'll make new friends.

And when their wives came to join them—or their sisters, to make good wives for other men—then the reasons for staying outweighed those for returning. Having settled down as Americans, the Lebanese immigrants wanted to bring more members of their families here rather than return home themselves.

Thus Lebanese immigrants, of the past and today, present an unusual picture of mixed attitudes and emotions. They loved the old country with enduring affection, for, except at times of stress, it was a good place to live and its beauties were fondly remembered.

4
NEW LIVES IN A NEW HOME

By the early 1900s, the Lebanese had joined the many other groups of immigrants who made their homes in the crowded neighborhoods of New York City.

Lebanese Settlements in America

New York—"al Na-Yurk"—was the stepping stone for most Lebanese immigrants, and for a large number, it also became their new home. In 1895, the popular magazine *Harper's Weekly* published an article about New York City's Lebanese community, describing its inhabitants in colorful and sympathetic terms. Some of the women proudly displayed high-fashion dresses and hats, while others still wore the traditional head scarves; the dark-eyed children were alert and beautiful; the men, some in red, brimless tarbooshes and some in top hats, could be seen playing backgammon at the Lebanese restaurants and smoking water pipes in front of their homes.

From the earliest days, however, many immigrants did not stay in New York but moved on to other places.

Some settled in Boston and other cities in the northeastern states. The real pioneers headed west and south—to Ohio, Michigan, North Dakota, Texas. Once an individual was established in some corner of the country, other members of his family or people from his village would naturally come to join him. By 1919, it is said, hardly a town of over 5,000 anywhere in the United States lacked a Lebanese family. Usually, at least a few families settled down together, but some were "rugged individualists" and preferred to be by themselves.

Since people from the same villages and generally the same religious sect tended to stick together, they recreated in the new country some of the characteristics of their village life in the old. For instance, if the village had had a good school, the immigrants would be likely to place a high value on education. On the other hand, religious and family quarrels also made the transfer and caused friction for as long as the first-generation settlers wanted to keep them alive.

Earning a Living

How did the early immigrants make the money that they so proudly sent home? The working lives of the Lebanese pioneers make a fascinating story, for their experiences were very different from those of many other ethnic groups.

Though most were rural people, in the United States, they were not attracted to farming. The plantation and sharecropping systems in the South were contrary to the Lebanese tradition of small, independently owned plots of land. Nor did the Lebanese want to break new ground and establish large farms in the Midwest, widely separated from neighbors. They were villagers and wanted to be close to other people. Thus only a few early immigrants took advantage of America's cheap farm land. Farm laborers were even fewer.

Just as they looked away from the farming that was the choice of so many European immigrants, the Lebanese also rejected the work that employed countless other newcomers: mining and factory labor. Given a choice, they had no interest in heavy industry, and very rare was the Lebanese immigrant who went underground. To work away from fresh air, just one of a throng under an indifferent or harsh boss, was a bad fate in their eyes. In short, they simply did not want to work for other people. Yet for the most part, the Lebanese newcomers were very poor and needed jobs desperately . . . so what sort of work was left for them?

Trading. The heritage of the Phoenicians emerged once more, and the mountain farmers became traders overnight. Though they would never have dreamed of doing it in their own country, here they worked as peddlers. They hoisted packs on their backs, picked up a suitcase in each hand, and set off to make a living by selling goods from door to door.

While some other immigrant groups also peddled in their early years in the United States, no other group claimed this way of making a livelihood as did the Lebanese. Probably some 90 percent of the immigrants who arrived before 1914 peddled for at least a short while. They earned a small but picturesque place in American folklore, as we can see in the Arab peddler who walks through the scenes of the ever-popular musical *Oklahoma!*

Very soon a Lebanese peddling network stretched over much of this vast country. Suppliers established themselves in many different centers. Fort Wayne, Indiana, for example, was a major one in the early years. Receiving shipments from Lebanese wholesalers in New York, the suppliers would distribute the goods to the peddlers in their areas. The local supplier played a varied role, using the labor of the peddlers but also looking after their needs. He often provided housing, advice, companionship, and "banking" services, saving and sending home the peddlers' money for them. Each depended on the other, but it was a purely voluntary arrangement.

The system worked well. A young Lebanese man just off the boat knew that he would be met by someone from his family or village and either taken to a place in New York or sent off to another destination. There he would be given a peddling pack and put on the road the next day. Sometimes the established merchants or suppliers would advance money for the newcomers'

In the movie version of the musical Oklahoma!, *actor Eddie Albert played the Arab peddler who sold his wares to the ranchers and farmers of the territory.*

A 14-year-old Lebanese peddler in Worcester, Massachusetts, poses with his case of wares (left) and his valise. Carrying such heavy burdens, peddlers walked hundreds of miles.

passage and then get them started as peddlers. As many as 50 young people at a time might come from a village and fit right into a well-organized business.

The peddlers usually started out on foot, going door-to-door all over the city and out to the suburbs. Those who went to rural areas hiked long distances from town to town, from farm to farm, from state to state. If they could not return at night to a peddlers' settlement in a town, the rural peddlers had no place to sleep. They depended on the kindness of country people for a good meal and a night's shelter. It was a hard life, requiring great strength and determination. But the peddlers kept at it, hoping to save enough to send some money home, or possibly to buy a horse and wagon to make their work easier.

At first the Lebanese peddlers sold mostly objects of olive wood and mother-of-pearl, religious items, fine laces and embroideries from Lebanon, Syria, and Palestine. These goods, associated with the Holy Land and not available in stores, were popular with Americans. They were usually of fine quality and brought a touch of exotic beauty to many lives. Soon, more everyday goods were added to the peddlers' packs—shoelaces, tools, kitchen implements, fabric, knives—all sorts of things that could be carried and that would be needed in people's homes.

Many Americans had mixed attitudes toward peddling, regarding it as low-status work for "desperate" people. Yet it was obviously needed! The peddlers provided a highly useful service. They were especially welcome in the homes of factory workers whose long hours left little time to shop and of farm families who could seldom get to even a small store.

In rural areas, the peddlers not only supplied people with needed items but also added some spice to their lives and brought contact with the world beyond the isolated farms. If they were sometimes chased by dogs and regarded with suspicion, they were far more often received well and welcomed back year after year. The peddlers took pride in

what they were doing and, years later, were much more likely to recall the funny and exciting incidents than the hardships.

Benefits to the Lebanese peddlers from their work were two-fold. They earned good money—often $10 to $12 a week, or even $5 a day. Around the turn of the century, this was a very respectable amount, much better than a factory worker could earn. Just as important, the peddlers got to know the United States and its citizens in a short time. They were forced to go out and meet people, interact with different kinds of people, become familar with American ways and values, and learn the language in a hurry. Most immigrant workers in factories and mines did not have these experiences.

Peddling meant independence, freedom, self-reliance—all values that the Lebanese immigrants brought with them. But of course peddling was not an end in itself. The early immigrants saw it as the quickest way to make money so that they could return to Lebanon and live comfortably. The fact that it was transient work, requiring no fixed address or community, was one of the attractions of peddling.

But in a sense, the peddlers' early expectations backfired. By acquainting them with the country and the people, peddling made it easier for them to feel like Americans themselves and to want to settle down. By trying to stay footloose, they hastened the process of putting down roots.

By the time of World War I, the ped-

If a peddler was successful, he eventually acquired a horse and wagon, like this Lebanese immigrant in Massachusetts. The dream of most peddlers was to leave traveling behind and start a small business.

dlers were settling down all over the country. Typically, they opened small stores, selling dry goods, groceries, or clothing. These were usually family concerns, and all members of the family worked. Having avoided jobs in which they would have to work for "bosses," the Lebanese also distrusted partners. Therefore they formed partnerships with the people they could trust most:

the members of their families.

Before long, some enterprising Lebanese owned factories that manufactured clothing, silk fabric, gloves, hats. Fortunes were being made even in the first years of this century. Because of the traditions of silk cultivation, fine weaving, and needlework in the old country, lingerie and linens were a specialty of many Lebanese stores.

In the early 1900s, the Abraham family owned and managed this department store in Canadian, Texas.

One rather surprising item manufactured in both homes and factories and featured in Lebanese-owned stores was the silk kimono. This Japanese-style garment was popular as a lounging robe in the early decades of the 20th century. By the 1920s, Lebanese entrepreneurs had 35 kimono factories in and near New York City and 25 silk factories in Paterson, New Jersey.

The typical route for most of the early immigrants, therefore, was this: peddling, small store, larger store—and, for a few, big business and even millionaire status. There were, of course, some variations on the theme. In the eastern states such as Massachusetts and New York, a number of immigrants did take factory jobs. They worked in the garment industry, also in brickmaking and cigarette factories, and even, in Pittsburgh, in the steel mills. In Fall River, Massachusetts, most of the immigrants worked in the textile mills that flourished in the first three decades of this century. Another variation was found in Maine, where some immigrants went to work in the lumber industry.

Almost universally, though, factory jobs were seen as short-term, simply the means to earn money to get started in a more independent line of work. The children of the Lebanese immigrants in Fall River, for example, vowed that they would never work in the mills like their parents. Eventually, most did manage to set up small businesses of their own.

A few hard-headed newcomers, determined to make money fast in any

In 1920, Mansour Farah (left), a Lebanese immigrant in Texas, established a company that manufactured men's clothes. Today the Farah brand of clothing is sold throughout the world.

Today as in the past, many Lebanese Muslims in Dearborn, Michigan, work in the automobile industry.

way they could, chose more questionable routes. For example, a team of gamblers—one aged 15—gambled their way west. They ended up in a small mining town in Arizona where the railroad line stopped and set up a flourishing gambling hall. Soon they were joined by more serious-minded family members who established a highly respectable store.

For the Muslims who came soon after World War I, the typical story was different. Many were attracted to the automobile industry around Detroit, where Henry Ford had announced liberal hiring practices and a wage of $5 a day. Before long, a Lebanese Muslim community, mostly Shi'ite Muslims from south Lebanon, grew up in Dearborn near Detroit.

Because of their religion, the Muslim immigrants preferred to stick together rather than to mingle with other Americans and become part of American society. The impersonal setting of the factory, therefore, which required little contact with other workers, seemed to suit them better than peddling. To this day, many Lebanese-American Muslims (along with other Arabs) have stayed in the automotive industry, and Dearborn has the largest Arab Muslim community in the United States.

Another community of Muslims, many of them originally from Lebanon, is in Toledo, Ohio. Although not "pioneers," this group should be mentioned because of its unusual characteristics, strikingly different from the Dearborn community.

The major migration of Muslims to Toledo started around 1945, coming from other parts of the United States rather than from the old country. What attracted them was a particularly profitable business that one Muslim family already living in the city had started, more or less "by accident," as they explained it. It was the liquor business—an interesting choice, since their religion prohibits Muslims from drinking alcohol! But in Toledo they have prospered by selling liquor in bars, restaurants, and stores, all the while preserving their religious identity and values.

Becoming Americans

If a Lebanese immigrant himself did not achieve middle-class status, he and his wife made every effort to see that their children did. In almost every family, the second generation surpassed their parents in education and occupation. Besides selling and manufacturing, they went into import/export, banking and finance, teaching, travel services. Real estate is another area of enterprise that has always been important to Lebanese Americans. Owning property—both for homes and as an investment—was a high priority among a people who traditionally had owned their homes and small farms in Lebanon.

A form of enterprise particularly popular with Lebanese Americans is the restaurant business. In almost every city with an Arabic community, there is a Lebanese restaurant and perhaps a bakery as well. Lebanese food, with a wide variety of flavorful dishes, is one of the world's greatest cuisines.

The professions also attracted many Lebanese Americans. Although usually it was the children and grandchildren of immigrants who became doctors, lawyers, and scholars, some first-generation Lebanese made huge leaps. A well-known story is that of Dr. Michael Shadid, who came in 1890 after beginning his education at the American University of Beirut. A young man, he peddled until he had saved $5,000, then put himself through medical school. In time, Shadid became not only a well-respected doctor but also the founder of the first cooperative, low-cost hospital in the country (located in Elk City, Oklahoma.) Another interesting success story is that of the poet Kahlil Gibran, who came as a penniless young boy in 1895 and by his middle teens had a reputation in Boston as an artist.

The immigrants from this tiny Arab country turned out to be very much in tune with American ways and values. The Lebanese had an intense drive for independence, security, financial success, enterprise, and property ownership. Religious people, hard-working and willing to live simply, they were ready to move to wherever opportunities were richest. Thus they not only were attracted to the United States by the "American dream," but they also embodied that dream—and took it with them to every corner of the country.

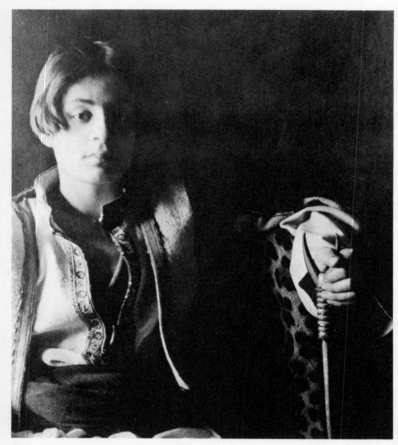

Kahlil Gibran

In 1895, 12-year-old Kahlil Gibran came to the United States with his mother, Kamila, his two sisters, and his stepbrother. The family settled with relatives in Boston, where Kahlil's developing skill as an artist attracted the attention of some influential people. The young immigrant was introduced to the literary and artistic world of Boston, and by the time he was 20, he had established a reputation as a promising artist. Gibran's stories and poems written in Arabic were also becoming known within the Arabic-speaking community in the United States as well as abroad.

In his later life, Kahlil Gibran continued to play an important role as a literary figure in the Arabic-speaking world. After 1918, however, he began to publish works written in English, and it is this part of his career that gave him lasting fame in the United States. Gibran's series of prose poems, *The Prophet,* which deals with such subjects as love, beauty, and death, has enjoyed tremendous popularity ever since its publication in 1923.

Opposite: *This photographic portrait of the young Kahlil Gibran was taken by the noted American photographer Fred Holland Day. Day was a friend and adviser during the early years of Gibran's career.*
Right: *This self-portrait of Kahlil Gibran appeared in a collection of Arabic stories published in 1908.*
Below: *A cover designed by Gibran for a publication of Arrabitah, a society of Arab-American writers*

{ جبران خليل جبران }

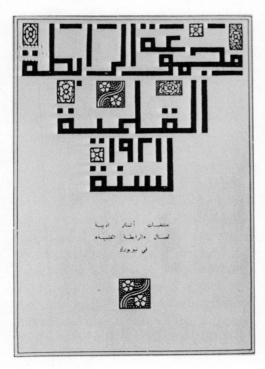

Kahlil Gibran died in 1931 and, in accordance with his wishes, was buried in Bsharri, the Lebanese village where he was born. His feelings about his homeland were expressed many years earlier when he wrote,

I am Lebanese and I'm proud of that,...
I have a beautiful homeland of which I'm proud,
And I have a nation with a past.
...No matter how many days I stay away
I shall remain an Easterner—Eastern in my manners,
Syrian in my desires, Lebanese in my feelings—
No matter how much I admire Western progress.

43

5
LEBANESE FLAVOR IN THE SALAD

Saadi Ferris, a Lebanese-American merchant in Austin, Texas, during the early 1900s

The United States has been called a "melting pot," a crucible where different elements are blended to become unified and alike. In some ways this is true, and Lebanese Americans certainly have done some "melting." Typically, immigrants and their children, once settled in this country, wanted to put aside their old ways and old identity and to think of themselves as 100-percent American.

But the distinctive qualities of different ethnic groups are what make American society lively and interesting. Perhaps a "tossed salad" might better describe the combining of things into an effective whole with the different ingredients still evident. With their dark coloring and their speech so different from English and European languages, what did the Lebanese add to the American "salad"?

What's in a Name?

First comes the question of the immigrants' basic identification—and this is something of a surprise. For a long time, they did not even exist, at least as "Lebanese." The term was simply not used. This was because Mount Lebanon had always been considered part of geographic Syria—with a separate history, to be sure, but not a separate national status.

If the people from Mount Lebanon thought of themselves as coming from a particular country, they called themselves Syrians. More often, though, they identified with their religious group: "I am Maronite," or "I am Orthodox." Then they described themselves by their villages: "I am from Majayoun," or "I am from Shweir." And most of all, they thought of themselves in terms of family. For three or four decades, therefore, national origin was not important or even a reality to these immigrants.

American immigration officials were equally unsure—or careless. The early immigrants were sometimes recorded as "Turks" because their country was then a part of the Ottoman Turkish

Officials at Ellis Island were often unsure about the name of the country from which Lebanese immigrants came. The immigrants' personal names, written in the unfamiliar language of Arabic, were another source of confusion.

empire. Or they might have been entered in the record book as "Greeks" because they were Christians from the eastern end of the Mediterranean, and "Greek" was a familiar term. Some were even called "Armenians" or "Assyrians." From 1899 on, however, the classification "Syrian" was used, along with these other labels.

Only in the mid-1920s, after Lebanon had become a republic, did the idea spread that the Lebanese were different from other Arabs. The Arabic press in New York campaigned to make the term "Lebanese" accepted. Around 1930, people in both the old country and the new began to call themselves "Lebanese."

Because the early records are so confused due to the changing terminology, it is impossible to determine accurately how many people immigrated from the land now called Lebanon. One fact, however, is certain: although the Arabic-speaking immigrants were mostly called "Syrians" for the first 50 years or so, the great majority of them were in fact from what is now Lebanon.

Besides the confusion over their identity as an ethnic group, the Lebanese in America faced another question of identity: their personal names. Many, of course, kept the Arabic names. Because Arabic is written in an alphabet totally different from English, however, spellings of the same name often differ. The name Khouri (which means "priest") can be spelled in such variations as Khoury, Khuri, Couri, Koory, and Corey.

Many people changed their names to the English equivalent in meaning or sound. The common name Haddad, for example, became the even commoner "Smith," and Ashshi became "Cook." Dark-eyed, olive-skinned people now bear the typical English names of Sawyer, Thomas, Joseph, George, and Abbott—formerly Sawaya, Tuma, Yusuf, Jirjus, and Abboud.

One Lebanese woman acquired a new name in a different way. Arriving in Maine around Christmastime, she was frequently greeted with "Merry Christmas!" Since her first name was Mary, she at first thought people were addressing her personally—and therefore decided that her new name would be "Mary Christmas."

Fitting In

The Lebanese, who were, of course, very few in number compared with other immigrant groups, met little discrimination or opposition in their new home. But inevitably there was some. If they were criticized in the early days, it was often from envy—they made such good money at their peddling. Sometimes, in poor sections of the cities, they were referred to disparagingly as "Turks" by people who did not understand that they were Christians and from a very different place and culture.

In October 1905, New York papers reported a street fight among "Syrians," dramatizing it with such terms as "swarthy" and "knife-wielding." The fight, which was quickly subdued, had blown up over the qualifications of a bishop! Quarrels among different Christian groups and religious factions, a hold-over from the old country, were about the only source of unrest among Lebanese immigrants in the early years.

In 1902, an American who had been a teacher in Lebanon, annoyed over criticisms of the Lebanese immigrants, sought to answer the critics scientifically. Analyzing the New York Lebanese colonies in terms of education, occupation, cleanliness, church-going, and family life, he published a book demonstrating they were among the most desirable of all ethnic communities.

It was not long, in fact, before the Lebanese in American towns and cities had an enviable reputation as law-abiding, productive citizens. Though sometimes their family and religious celebrations were noisy, as had been the custom in villages at home, they avoided rowdiness, drunkenness, and crime. A strong concept of family honor and avoidance of shame kept people in line.

Likewise, the religious group provided firm guidelines for behavior. Bringing shame to the family and the religious community would cut a person off from the group, and very few were willing to pay that price. Thus the Lebanese newcomers, the majority of whom were young unmarried men, stayed out of trouble and buckled down to the business of earning money.

Moreover, the Lebanese had an open

Like many Lebanese immigrants, Joe Azar Youness (right) and his cousin Joe Youness were young men who came to seek their fortunes in the United States. The cousins emigrated to North Dakota in 1898.

47

and positive attitude toward the new country. Many stayed in the major urban centers such as New York and Detroit, but the remarkable thing is that so many were willing to go anywhere and everywhere in the country that opportunity might lead them. They were willing to try their luck in just about any spot where their trading talents and other abilities might bear fruit. And they enthusiastically and ceaselessly praised the United States as the land of opportunity for all.

Desire for education, which began in Lebanon in the early 19th century, also strengthened Lebanese newcomers in the United States. Although the majority were illiterate or little educated when they arrived, they tried their best to learn as much as they could. They made certain that their children had schooling as soon as they settled down—as much education as possible for their sons and, in some cases, for their daughters. The conviction that education leads to success is one of the most striking features of the Lebanese both in this country and in Lebanon.

RASHID FAMILY REUNIO

This photograph was taken at the annual reunion of the Rashid family held in Chicago on July 4, 1985. Today fewer than five percent of the 2,500 family members

A Distinctive Flavor
Family Life

Lebanese immigrants fit easily into American society, but at the same time, they maintained a sense of distinctiveness. The family was—and is—the first line of a separate Lebanese identity. From the early years, many members of a family would come to the United States, often at different times, and live close together. If they eventually scattered around the country, they kept track of one another.

This is still true today. For example, the Rashid family, whose members live all over the United States, estimate their present numbers at 2,500. Since 1972, they have had an annual reunion, usually in an eastern or midwestern city, with about 600 to 700 currently attending. The Rashids also have a scholarship fund to help family members in Lebanon.

Another close-knit family are the Aboul-Hosns from the village of Btekhnay. Coinciding with the annual con-

were born in Lebanon, and names such as McCallister and Kowolski are common in the family directory. At the annual reunion, however, everyone is a Rashid.

49

vention of the American Druze Society, they hold a three-day family reunion with close to 100 adults and children attending. The Aboul-Hosns have also compiled a family directory; one-third of the listed members are in the health fields, engineering, and computer technology.

Family ties among Lebanese are still strong, but there have been some changes in recent years. The early immigrants almost always married women from Lebanon, preferably from their own villages. In succeeding generations, however, young Lebanese Americans have been much more willing to marry outside of their community, including people of different religions. Thus family ties may be said to be both widening and becoming weaker.

Religion

Religion has been another distinctive element in the lives of the Lebanese immigrants. Wherever enough Christian Lebanese and Syrians settled, they soon started churches of their respective faiths—Maronite, Melkite, or Orthodox. The church provided, and continues to provide, an important focus for the lives of individuals and the community. Many Maronite and Melkite churches, however, have undergone significant change in their ritual and language, for example, substituting English and Latin for the traditional Arabic or Syriac in their services. Because of such changes, the churches seem to be losing their

Archbishop Francis M. Zayek is the head of the Maronite Church in the United States.

distinctive character and becoming increasingly like the American Roman Catholic Church.

Over the years, this change has caused concern in some communities among those who want to preserve the traditions and rituals of the old religious forms and not be swallowed up in sameness. Other Lebanese people, however, insist that since they are now Americans, their churches should also be Americanized. The problem has been less noticeable in the Orthodox churches because of the Orthodox tradition of adopting the local language of the people.

Our Lady of Perpetual Help in Worcester, Massachusetts, is a Melkite church attended by Lebanese Americans. Melkite services include some of the elaborate ceremonies typical of Eastern Christian churches throughout the world.

Lebanese Muslim immigrants faced greater difficulties in adapting to the American scene. Not only did they find no mosque or much understanding of their religion, but their religious practices sometimes conflicted with American ways. The requirement of mid-day prayer in a clean place, for example, could not easily be met in a factory. Foods prepared according to Muslim law (for example, meat from animals slaughtered in a certain way) were not available in most places. American laws concerning marriage, inheritance, and other personal matters also conflicted with Islamic law, which devout Muslims believe to be God's word.

Whereas Lebanese Christians could go to American churches if they wished, Muslims had to establish their own places of worship, and they could not do so until they formed sufficiently large communities. By 1919, enough Muslims had settled in Highland Park, near Detroit, to create a mosque. It had to be sold soon afterward because of maintenance costs, but a second mosque was established in Michigan City, Indiana, in 1924 and has been in use ever since. Today there are mosques and Islamic centers in several major cities across the country.

In time, as with the Christian communities, many children of Muslim immigrants became Americanized and lost interest in religious practices that set them apart from other people. But today, with the growth of Islamic fundamentalism in the Middle East and also in the United States, the question of how

Muslims praying in a Dearborn, Michigan, mosque. Faithful Muslims pray five times each day, facing in the direction of the holy city of Mecca.

Lebanese and other Arabs of Islamic faith fit into American society is far from a dead issue.

Other Community Institutions

Besides family and church, Lebanese Americans have maintained a sense of community through business connections. In the early days, traders and businessmen felt comfortable doing business with their countrymen, whose methods and manners they understood—and whose cousins they might be married to. In general, they preferred to find ways to cooperate rather than compete. Since a large proportion of Lebanese Americans went into business of many kinds and in all parts of the country, it was quite natural that they should help each other and, when possible, seek mutually beneficial arrangements. This goes on today, demonstrating continued responsibility toward relatives and friends, especially those recently arrived from Lebanon.

Early Lebanese immigrants brought not only their trading skills and determination to work hard but also a concern for their language and literature. Soon Arabic newspapers and literary journals were flourishing in New York City. As the Lebanese and Syrians spread far and wide throughout the country, they depended on the Arabic press to help them keep in touch with the old country and with each other. By 1905 there were 13 newspapers; in 1929 the total number of Arabic newspapers and magazines that had been started in the United States was calculated at 102. Though many of the publications came to a natural end, especially as people became educated in English and more American in their attitudes, one, *Al-Hoda*, has published continuously since 1898.

Another group concerned with the Arabic language was a society of Lebanese and Syrian writers called the Pen League. The league was established in New York City in 1920 and centered around the poet and artist Kahlil Gibran and the writer Ameen Rihany. One of its primary aims was the revitalizing of Arabic language and literature. This society had a significant effect on the literary revival in the Arab countries that took place in the early 1900s.

Clubs have always been a center of social life among the Lebanese Americans. Enthusiastic organizers, the immigrants soon formed associations in different cities—as early as the 1890s in New York. Today, Lebanese/Syrian associations exist in almost every state under such names as the West Georgia Cedars, the Ladies' Cedars Club, the Lebanese Athletic League. Though some may have a charitable purpose, they are primarily social clubs. The annual convention of the Midwestern Federation of Syrian-Lebanese Clubs, for example, is a gala affair. Held in a different city each year, the gathering is often attended by whole families, some of whom may come with hopes of finding a suitable marriage partner for a son or daughter.

Members of the American-Lebanese Men's Club in Minneapolis, Minnesota, pose for a group photo in the 1920s.

The Druze have also maintained a few associations for Lebanese and Syrian Americans of the Druze faith. Many other groups include people of varied Arab backgrounds, such as Islamic organizations (Islam being a faith that emphasizes universality) and those with a professional, educational, or political purpose. The Arab American Medical Association is one example.

Although Lebanese Americans have always associated with other Americans freely in business, school, civic affairs, and organizations such as the Masons, they have often preferred to keep to themselves socially. Thus their clubs, for many years, both gave them a stronger group feeling and tended to isolate them from the larger community.

This suggests one criticism that has been made of many Lebanese-American communities. At least in the past, their members stayed together too much and restricted their social contacts to people of the same religious group. This attitude reduced their interaction not only with other Americans but also with other Lebanese and Syrians.

Among the Lebanese of Boston, for

example, there was little contact or cooperation between people of different sects and little sense of unity in a broader Lebanese or Arab community with common interests. Christians overemphasized their differences and their separateness from other Christians—and, even more so, from other Arabs. Whereas families took care of their relatives admirably and churches provided welfare for their members in need, concern did not extend beyond these narrowly defined limits.

These attitudes, fortunately, now seem to be giving way to growing awareness of the need for a stronger and more united Lebanese-American community, one that is better able to demonstrate concern for the old country in its present troubles.

Moreover, there are many examples of efforts by Lebanese communities to encourage interest in their ethnic characteristics not only among their members but also among the broader American public. Occasionally, a Lebanese-American church or community will hold a large festival. In Toledo, Ohio, for example, the two Orthodox churches of Saint Elias and Saint George each sponsor a Syrian-Lebanese-American festival annually, both of them well

The Flowers of Arabia Dabke Troupe performs traditional Arabic dances at cultural events in the Detroit area. The canes that the group members are holding in this photograph are used in the dabke *(or* debki), *which is a spirited line dance.*

attended by the general public as well as the Arab community. Lebanese food, costumes, music, and crafts are featured at such events as well as lots of dancing—the rhythmic group dance known as the *debki* and sometimes even the exciting and difficult sword dance.

Another popular type of event that often cuts across religious differences is the *mahrajan,* a kind of festive picnic. The first one was held in Bridgeport, Connecticut, in 1930, and now such gatherings occur in communities all over the country. The *mahrajan* provides an opportunity for families to enjoy food, music, and dancing and for young people to meet each other. The Lebanese value social events like this as a means of strengthening ethnic identity and of keeping traditions alive among the upcoming generations.

A store owner in Detroit cutting a piece of halawah. *This sweet made from sesame is very popular among Lebanese Americans and others of Middle Eastern ancestry.*

Lebanese Food

One Lebanese tradition, perhaps above all others, has helped maintain a Lebanese flavor in the American "tossed salad," and that, logically, is food. Even the generations who wanted to suppress their ethnic background never forgot the Lebanese cuisine. Any gathering still brings out favorite traditional dishes such as felafil, kibbi, and tabbouli, many of them now favorites with other Americans as well. As long as the "Lebanese restaurant" remains a popular eating place in any town that has one, Lebanese Americans will probably be a distinctive ethnic community.

Conflicting Values

Newcomers from Lebanon had little difficulty fitting into American society for several reasons: their limited numbers, their independence and drive to get ahead, their readiness to make the most of what the United States had to offer them, and their strong social values. They were very quick to become solid middle-class citizens.

In some respects, however, traditional Lebanese values conflicted with American ways. In the United States, children were given much more freedom than was common in Lebanon. Lebanese families had to come to terms with the privileges granted not only children but

56

also women, plus the lessening of the father's power as undisputed head of the household. Daughters of immigrant families had to be granted a somewhat freer social life than they would have had in the old country.

Many Lebanese newcomers have also found it difficult to accept the typical American attitude toward hospitality. People in the United States do not visit frequently and easily in cafes and in each others' homes (without invitation), the way they do in the Middle East.

Nonetheless, the traditional Lebanese emphasis on the family has helped many Lebanese Americans to withstand the stresses of social change. To this day, they continue to be relatively conservative, family-oriented people, high-achieving and hard working, whose niche in the American scene is respected and secure.

Hospitality is an important part of Lebanese culture. The women in a family are usually responsible for serving food to guests and visiting relatives.

6
LEBANESE WOMEN IN AMERICA

Eva Habib was employed in the Detroit automobile industry during the 1920s. Her grimy overalls suggest that she worked hard for a living.

The typical Western view of Middle Eastern women—at least in the past—pictured lives of seclusion and oppression. No doubt, some women in 19th-century Lebanon did lead idle, confined existences, especially those in well-to-do city families. But this was not true in the villages.

Although most village women had no options other than home-making, they had complete charge of the home, a role considered almost "sacred" in Lebanese culture. Their abilities were highly respected, and they developed many skills. Despite the husband's final authority, the wife also had a voice in family affairs and was not afraid to use it.

In the last decades of the 19th century, the position of women in Lebanese society was also being influenced by the fact that increasing numbers of girls were going to the schools founded by mission groups in many villages. By the time emigration started, therefore, some Lebanese women and girls were ready to think about their own places in the modern world. They knew that they came behind the menfolk, to be sure, but they stood with considerable strength of their own. The long tradition of liberty in the mountain undoubtedly encouraged this attitude.

Women Who Emigrated

In the early days, almost all Lebanese emigrants were men. As those men decided to stay on in the United States, naturally they began to think of family life, so important in Arab culture. They wanted the comforts of home; they wanted wives. The married ones brought their families to America, while single men often returned briefly to their villages to find brides. Any unmarried Lebanese woman who came to this country could be sure of being sought after. Sometimes marriages were arranged, and a girl would be sent to the United States to be the wife of an immigrant already settled here.

The men wanted wives to keep house and prepare good Lebanese food for them, of course. But wives and daughters were also a major economic asset. Any businessman, whether peddler or factory owner, needed completely trustworthy partners in his work, and the women of the family fit that description.

Though probably most women immigrants had some male family member waiting for them in America, a surprising number came on their own. They,

A young Lebanese woman (left), newly married and headed for the United States, poses for a shipboard photo with a friend.

too, were determined to find a better life for themselves and their children. It was not unknown for married women to pack up and leave their husbands and even their children behind in the village! While probably not a common situation, a mother might choose to go to America instead of her adult son, sending money home to make life easier for him and his family.

Zimrod and Elias Razook

Zimrod Razook was the first of a family of Lebanese women who emigrated to the United States on their own. In 1889, Zimrod, a widow, came to North Dakota with her son, Elias. She established a homestead in the town of Rugby and worked as a midwife until her death in 1915.

In 1898, Zimrod's daughter, Natalia Razook Saliba (seated in the photograph at the right), also emigrated to North Dakota. She left behind in Lebanon her husband, Anton Saliba (seated next to Natalia), a stepson, Ferris (standing, center), and two daughters, Lillian (left) and Zachia (right). Like her mother, Natalie homesteaded land in Rugby. She became a naturalized American citizen in 1903 and, three years later, returned to Lebanon to be with her family. After Anton Saliba died in 1908, Natalie came back to North Dakota with her two young daughters.

The Saliba family

Lillian and Zachia Saliba

Lillian and Zachia Saliba grew up in the little town of Rugby. To help out family finances, the two girls did needlework and sold it door to door. In 1915, Lillian married Tom Nassif, also an immigrant from Lebanon.

Zachia's wedding picture

Hazel Azar

Zachia, nicknamed Zachey, married in 1913 (above), at the age of 16. Her husband was Joe Azar Youness, who had come to North Dakota from the Lebanese village of Zahle in 1898. Zachey's daughter Hazel (left) represented the first American-born generation of this family of strong women.

Kamila Gibran (left) came to the United States in 1895 with her four children, including daughters Sultana (center) and Marianna (right). This striking photograph of the three women was taken by Fred Holland Day in 1901.

children and came to the United States. Settling with the Lebanese community in Boston, she promptly put together a pack of goods and went out to peddle. By her hard work she made a new life for her family and enabled her son to find the opportunities and the friends who would later bring him recognition.

Emigration often caused major changes in relationships between the sexes and within Lebanese families. No longer so subordinate, women in families where the men had gone overseas now had prestige from the money sent home and more authority as acting heads of households. Even more so, those women who went to America themselves gained independence. By 1895, as many women as men in certain villages were leaving for America—sometimes even more. Of course, too, as villages emptied of young men, some girls had to follow them to the New World in hopes of finding a husband with the right religious, family, and village background.

Kamila Gibran, independent-spirited mother of the famous writer Kahlil, was one of those Lebanese women who emigrated on their own. In 1895, when her husband's unwise activities led him to disgrace, she left the remote mountain village of Bsharri with her four

Women's Work

Lebanese women in the United States played a very important role in the economic life of the immigrant communities. In the early years, some women took jobs in factories, especially silk and clothing manufacture. Later, those with enough schooling could find employment in, for example, nursing and social work. The majority, however, went on the road at first. Like

Kamila Gibran, they shouldered a pack and set off to work as peddlers.

Women peddlers were often welcomed into American homes more readily than men since many of the items sold, such as underwear and delicate fabrics, were considered more appropriately handled by women. Thus they were often more successful than the men. The criticism was even made that those "lazy Syrians" sent their wives out to work while staying home themselves, but in actual fact, both men and women seem to have worked hard and cooperatively.

The peddler's life of loneliness and self-reliance was a drastic reversal of the kind of existence that Lebanese women and girls had always known. At home, even while working hard, they had had the protection of their families. Here they had to go out and face the world every day, depend on the good will and kindness of strangers, and get along under conditions of real hardship. But, just like the men, women peddlers were determined to work for the dual goals of helping their families at home and realizing a more comfortable future life.

If they themselves did not peddle, wives often made small articles of clothing, as well as Arabic bread and sweets, for their husbands to sell. When families reached the point where they could start a store or a business, the partnership between husband and wife was one of equality or close to it.

The following story illustrates the resourcefulness of many Lebanese women immigrants in earning a living and making their own way. A 12-year-old girl, Helen Mousa Elias, came alone to the United States right after World War I, expecting to be met in Cincinnati by her brother. By that time, however, he was peddling in Texas. When word reached him of his sister's arrival, he "peddled" his way back to Ohio on foot, a journey of three months.

Meanwhile, the girl was selling chewing gum at movie theaters during the day and going to school at night to learn English. Then, still a teenager, she started reading about business management. Soon she bought a small grocery with living quarters above it and, later in life, sold insurance from her home. When she died in the 1970s, this woman left a flourishing insurance business to her son.

A Freer Life?

The greater freedom permitted Lebanese women in American society naturally encouraged higher expectations than they would have had in the old country. In New York during the 1890s, for example, those young women who could afford it quickly adopted the latest American fashions and took pride in their stylish appearance. Along with the new clothes, but acquired more gradually, came a greater independence of action.

The economic power of women contributed to this independence. As husbands depended more and more on

In 1912, Sadie Ray, an immigrant from Lebanon, won first prize for the best carriage in a parade held in Bangor, Maine.

their wives' money-making abilities, they had to share some authority, too. Women's roles began to change, and they gained power in the family—disciplining of children, for one thing—and a more forceful role in community affairs.

For many young women, however, the hopes encouraged by the "American dream" were not realized. Even more than in the old country, they were expected to work for their families. From the early teens, girls helped in the store and in the home, working such long hours that they sometimes had to give up going to school. They sacrificed their own hopes for those of the men in the family, even postponing marriage

until, in the eyes of Lebanese society, they were "too old."

The demands of working outside the home, which was the choice or fate of the majority of Lebanese women immigrants, meant a double burden on wives. The traditional Arabic emphasis on hospitality and frequent social visiting required, of course, a constant supply of good food—and who prepared the food but the wife and mother of the family? A woman thus had an indispensable social role, which was hard to combine with working hours as long as those of the husband, plus the demands of home-making and child-raising.

This dilemma naturally forced some practical changes in most families.

Above: *In the 1920s, Zachey and Joe Azar managed their own candy store in Bismark, North Dakota.* Right: *Thirty years later, Zachey (center) was still employed, working as a waitress in a waffle shop owned by the Azar family.*

Cooking had to be simplified and the preparation of time-consuming dishes saved for festive occasions. The traditional custom of visiting without notice had to be altered and social visits more often arranged in advance.

Whether or not able to acquire education themselves, Lebanese-American women have always been ambitious for their children, urging them to gain as much education as possible. The schooling of daughters, however, was not often considered as important as that of sons. For example, in the large Lebanese-Syrian community of Detroit during the early 1930s, where many young men were going to college, only two girls received college degrees. In this respect, of course, the Lebanese Americans were not very different from the broader American society. Moreover, there were always some families who encouraged daughters to go as far in their education as they wished.

By the 1950s, the days when many girls expected to sacrifice themselves for their families were past. Women of Lebanese background were asserting themselves in education, business, the professions, and public affairs. There are numerous instances of wives working in their husbands' businesses as top executives. Today Lebanese-American women are in every way as involved in the "work world" as any women in American society, and vigorously active in cultural, political, and philanthropic organizations. In fact, they have a great advantage in the strong drive for achievement and the close emotional

Lois DeBakey

support that characterize Lebanese-American families.

A few examples of Lebanese-American women prominent in their fields are Donna Shalala, president of Hunter College, New York City; Lois DeBakey, who is professor of scientific communication at Baylor College of Medicine; and Laura Nader, professor of anthropology at the University of California, Berkeley. Doctors DeBakey and Nader are members of families where high achievement is the norm; both have brothers who are eminent in their respective fields.

In Washington, D.C., Salwa Showker Roosevelt serves as Chief of Protocol at the White House, and Alixa Naff is di-

Salwa Showker Roosevelt

rector of the Arab-American Archives at the Smithsonian Institution. Also in the nation's capital, Helen Khal, a painter, has written extensively on contemporary art in the Arab world, with special focus on women artists. One of the notable Lebanese women who have immigrated to the United States in recent years is Dr. Hind Shuman Teixidor, professor of radiology and mammography at Cornell University Medical Center in New York City.

Today the traditional Arabic saying, "A girl is good in the house and in the field," is still true—but with new meaning. Lebanese women still value their roles as homemaker, cook, and hostess. But "in the field" now means whatever field of activity they choose, and there they also excel.

7
SOME LEBANESE AMERICANS OF NOTE

Michael DeBakey

Once the peddling days were past, people of Lebanese background began to move into an impressive range of careers and occupations. Their contributions to this country are out of all proportion to their small numbers.

Medicine

Medicine has long been an area where people of Arab cultures have excelled. During the Middle Ages, in fact, physicians in the Arab countries were far ahead of Europeans in their scientific and medical knowledge. This tradition continues; Lebanese-American doctors became noted for their achievements at least as early as 1940.

Today Dr. Michael DeBakey, a pioneer in open-heart surgery in the 1960s, is one of the most eminent men in his field. He pursues his work at Baylor College of Medicine in Houston, Texas, after a lifetime of distinction in research and surgery. Specialized care for wounded servicemen is another of his concerns, as is the training of young doctors and public policy affecting health care.

Government and Public Service

Law, like medicine and scholarship, is another career highly favored by Lebanese. This background often leads to careers in government and public health affairs. In the late 1970s, Philip Habib, a career diplomat, was in the news frequently as he represented the United States in Middle Eastern negotiations concerning the war in Lebanon. In recent years, he has served as the president's personal representative in such trouble spots as Central America and the Philippines. Najeeb Halaby served as head of the Federal Aviation Agency from 1960 to 1965 and then became chief executive of Pan American World Airways. Since 1973, he has been president of a corporation specializing in Third World development projects.

Several Lebanese Americans have been elected to the United States Senate. James Abourezk (South Dakota) served from 1972 to 1979 and is now an attorney active in Arab-American

Above: *Philip Habib is a career diplomat who has played an important role in Middle East negotiations.* Below: *Nick Rahall has represented West Virginia in the United States Congress since 1976.*

69

Victor Atiyeh

George Latimer

political affairs. James Abdnor (South Dakota) and George Mitchell (Maine) were both elected for six-year terms in 1981. United States Representatives include Mary Rose Oakar, Congresswoman from Cleveland, Ohio, serving from 1977 to the present; Nick Rahall, current Congressman from West Virginia, first elected to Congress in 1976 at age 27; Abraham Kazen, who represented his district in Texas from 1967 to 1984; and Toby Moffett, Congressman from Connecticut, 1975-82. The governor of Oregon, Victor Atiyeh, first elected in 1979, is from a Lebanese family. A businessman, he had earlier served in the state legislature for 20 years.

On the local level, Lebanese Americans have a much longer record in politics and community service. Peoria, Illinois, where the first Lebanese immigrants settled as early as 1885, presents an interesting illustration. With a Lebanese community accounting for only five percent of the population of 200,000, the people of Peoria have elected a mayor (James Maloof), a sheriff, and a city councilman of Lebanese background. Another midwestern city, St. Paul, Minnesota, has elected a mayor of Lebanese ancestry, George Latimer, for six consecutive terms, beginning in 1975.

Since the mid-1960s, Ralph Nader has been widely recognized as a defender of consumer and citizen rights. The Washington-based attorney, from a Lebanese family in Connecticut, first became known by challenging the safety of American automobiles. He continues to work for reform in big corporations, improved legislation, clean water, industrial safety, and other objectives that affect peoples' lives every day.

Prominent in public affairs from another angle is Helen Thomas, United Press International correspondent who often appears at presidential press conferences. She was the first woman to be appointed a White House correspondent and has effectively dealt with the last six presidents.

Scholarship

University and college faculties all over the country include many prominent professors of Lebanese background. Their fields range from literature and history to medicine and engineering.

The best known Lebanese scholar was Philip Hitti, whose career at Princeton and other leading universities spanned the years from 1916 to 1954. Hitti first came to the United States in 1913 as a very young man. In his lifetime of 92 years, he produced a wealth of scholarly work on Middle Eastern history and culture, and trained generations of younger scholars.

Another example of a first-generation "academic achiever" was Elias Sabbagh, who received one of the very first Ph.D's awarded in engineering by Purdue University in 1934. Dr. Sabbagh taught at Purdue from 1928 to 1970.

Above: *Ralph Nader talks to reporters at a Washington news conference.* Below: *Philip Hitti was a well-known scholar who specialized in Middle Eastern history and culture.*

Rosalind Elias has played many roles at the Metropolitan Opera, among them the menacing witch in Humperdincks' opera Hansel and Gretel.

The Arts and Entertainment

The world of the arts and entertainment boasts some stars of Lebanese background. Rosalind Elias made her debut at the Metropolitan Opera in 1954 and has sung leading roles for many years. Kahlil Gibran, godson and cousin of the famous writer, is a prominent sculptor in Boston and also co-author of an excellent biography of the poet. A much-published writer today is William Blatty, perhaps best known for his book *The Exorcist* and for the screenplay used in the film version of the book, both enormous popular successes.

One of this country's most enduring and best-loved popular entertainers is Danny Thomas, an actor and comedian on radio and television since the 1940s. Another of Mr. Thomas's roles is founder of the St. Jude Hospital in Memphis, Tennessee, which carries on cancer research and treats stricken children, often without charge to the patient's family. Mr. Thomas continues to raise money for this hospital, a project of particular interest to many Lebanese-American groups.

Above: *Sculptor Kahlil Gibran with his bronze statue* Lady of the Cedars, *created for the Cedars of Lebanon Church in Jamaica Plains, New York.* Below: *Danny Thomas with one of the young patients at the St Jude Hospital in Memphis, Tennessee.*

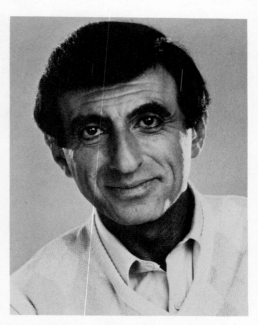

Above: *Marlo Thomas and Jamie Farr were both featured in long-running television series.*
Below: *The voice of Casey Kasem is familiar to music fans all over the United States.*

Danny's daughter, Marlo Thomas, is an actress who starred in a popular TV series, "That Girl," and has also been involved in the fashion industry. Jamie Farr—"Corporal Max Klinger"—was one of the crew in the long-running television series "M.A.S.H." Victor Tayback is another actor familiar from a popular television series, "Alice." Paul Anka has been composing hit songs since his teens and is also a singer and entertainer. "The most listened-to voice in America," according to one popular magazine, is that of Casey Kasem, host of major radio and TV music shows.

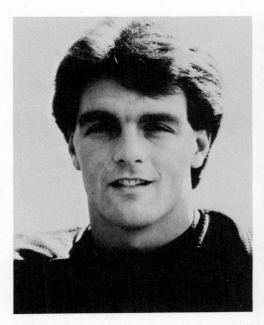

Doug Flutie was an outstanding football player at Massachusett's Boston College.

Sports

Though Lebanese Americans usually put their energies into business and the professions, there are some Lebanese names in professional athletics as well. Eddie Dibs is one, a high-ranking tennis player in the late 1970s. In football, Abe Gibron coached the Chicago Bears in the 1970s, and Bill George, who played for the Bears, is in professional football's Hall of Fame. Doug Flutie, 1984 winner of the Heisman Trophy, college football's most prestigious award, is also of Lebanese background.

After winning the Heisman Trophy in 1984, Doug Flutie played for one season with the New Jersey Generals in the United States Football League. When the league disbanded in 1986, Flutie was signed as a quarterback with the Chicago Bears, and his pro career was ready to take off.

The company established by Joseph Marion Haggar (above left and below) in the 1920s is today one of the world's largest producers of men's slacks, sport coats, and suits.

Business

In business and manufacturing, the names Haggar and Farah are familiar to most members of the American population who wear pants. Both of these Texas-based firms were founded by Lebanese entrepreneurs. The business started in 1926 by J. M. Haggar, immigrant from a small Lebanese village, has been described as the world's largest manufacturer of men's pants.

Ameen Haddad, now in his 80s, is known as "the potato king" in the U.S.

potato-growing and wholesaling business. On the other hand, a highly successful entrepreneur who refused to go "big" is Sam Maloof of California. This wood craftsman, whose furniture is displayed in the White House and in leading museums nationwide, designs and produces about 65 pieces a year entirely by hand. In 1985, he was awarded a $300,000 MacArthur Foundation fellowship to further artistic and philanthropical projects of his own choice.

Though other Lebanese-American business entrepreneurs are not so well known by name or "royal title," the list of men and women who have distinguished themselves in the corporate world is almost without end. Many have risen to the top in banking and finance. George Coury (whose father arrived in 1891 and walked all the way to Oklahoma as a peddler) became the first Arab-American member of the U.S. Stock Exchange. Another example is Robert Abboud, formerly a high executive of the First National Bank of Chicago and now president of Occident Petroleum Corporation.

Real estate, contracting, land development, and insurance are other fields in which many Lebanese Americans are active, reflecting the traditional importance of property ownership in the old country.

Well-known names illustrate the impact of this small immigrant population on American society. Also of great value have been the contributions of countless ordinary Lebanese Americans

Sam Maloof

in running their small businesses and pursuing their professions. They strengthen the communities where they live and raise families of future Lebanese-American citizens who embody the best qualities of both cultures. Not least important has been the readiness with which Lebanese Americans—in large numbers for the size of their community—have served in this country's armed forces since the First World War.

8
LINKS WITH THE OLD COUNTRY

A traditional Lebanese necklace adorns this young immigrant living in Utah.

From the beginning of Lebanese immigration to the United States, ties to the old country have been strong and enduring. During this 100-year period, however, the connections have undergone some significant changes.

The Early Years

How did the people at home feel about those who first left for the New World? In some countries from which emigrants departed, there was resentment, a feeling of being deserted. Not true in Lebanon! On the contrary, the folks at home were keenly interested in the emigrants' progress, which they knew would eventually bring benefit to them. Those who could, generally wanted to make the crossing themselves.

For their part, the immigrants expected to keep strong personal ties with the old country. Some, especially married men, went back repeatedly, only to return once more to the United States for another round of working and saving. One man made the trip between Peoria, Illinois, and his native village 19 times in 20 years, until the outbreak of World War I persuaded him to stay in America.

Once settled, as we have seen, the immigrants continued to send money home. The effect was soon highly visible. Better houses, especially ones with colorful red-orange tile roofs, began to spring up in villages all over the mountain. Each family wanted a larger house than the neighbors' as proof of how well its sons had done. But in many Lebanese villages, even today, houses can be seen with no roofs at all, their stone walls crumbling. These were the homes of owners who departed for the New World leaving no one behind to care for their property. Thus the effect of emigration on village life was not only advancement but also abandonment.

The improvement of property and of people's well-being far outweighed the losses, however. Emigrants were eager to help not only their own families but their villages as well, for villages, rather than country, held their loyalty and gave them identity. Thus churches were built and improved, schools were started, hospitals constructed, municipal buildings and monuments erected.

Zahle, now a sizeable city on the eastern slopes of the mountains, grew from a village of mud brick houses to

Photographs of the people back home kept emigrants in touch with their families and villages in Lebanon. This portrait, taken in the 1920s, shows the Noujain family from the village of Massar-el-Chouf.

a town of stone buildings in the 25 years after 1885. In 1911, the people of this town were receiving an average of $500 a day from their emigrants in the United States and other countries.

An American correspondent, visiting Lebanon in 1907 with the U.S. Immigration Commission, estimated that the Lebanese in America sent home more money per capita than any other immigrant group in the United States. During World War I, people continued to send money. Though often the funds never reached their destination, in many cases it was only these remittances that kept villagers alive.

Another dramatic example of support for the native village is the organization of emigrants from Kfeir. By now, about 900 families in North America trace their background to this small village. Every year since 1932, "Kfeirians" in the New World have held a reunion, rotating among eight cities of Ohio and West Virginia. Besides fellowship, they have created a foundation that has supported several projects in the village of Kfeir, such as water and electrical systems, a road, and a junior college.

The tradition of financial support for families and villages in Lebanon continues today. These funds have always been a significant part of the national income. The universities as well, particularly the American University of Beirut, depend heavily on gifts by emigrants. One indirect blow to Lebanon caused by the war that started in 1975 has been the reduction of money sent from abroad.

The American University of Beirut has received much financial support from Lebanese Americans.

Citizens of Two Countries

Generous financial contributions both to the old country and to institutions in the United States illustrate the "double loyalty" of many Lebanese Americans. Double loyalty takes another form as well. Lebanon is one of the few countries that permit dual citizenship. This means that a person who meets qualifications of birth or naturalization can be a citizen of both Lebanon and another country. An American child born in Beirut, for example, may have both Lebanese and American citizenship. A child born in the United States of a Lebanese father may likewise be entitled to passports from both countries.

This situation has served the interests of certain Christian political groups in Lebanon. By including people living in other countries in their numbers, they have sought to demonstrate the numerical strength of the Lebanese Christians. On the personal level, the arrangement permits some Lebanese people to leave

Both the Lebanese and the U. S. flags are displayed by a group of Lebanese Americans posing in front of the Al Hoda office building in New York City during the 1930s.

the country and settle elsewhere freely, without the complications of visas and immigration quotas.

In the case of Lebanese Americans, double allegiance has had a rather curious effect. The immigrants have always maintained a connection with Lebanon, but their intense loyalty to the United States has helped to insulate many against the storms affecting their original country. Lebanon is situated in the midst of one of the most turbulent parts of the world. The country bordering it on the south, Israel, has been in a state of hostility with the Arab countries since its creation in 1948 out of what had been the state of Palestine. When the uneasy relations between Israel and its Arab neighbors break into guerrilla attack, retaliation, and open warfare, as they have countless times, Lebanon is inevitably drawn into the trouble.

For many years, most Lebanese Americans did not take an active interest in Lebanon's problems. Business-oriented and politically conservative, Lebanese-American communities tended to focus on their own concerns. They did not express, on the national political level, views regarding Lebanon's welfare. Even less did the general social and political problems of the Arab world affect them.

Generally speaking, most Americans of Lebanese ancestry did not identify with the Arab cause or think of themselves as Arabs. Religious differences were part of the explanation. The great majority of Lebanese Americans, perhaps 90 percent, are Christian. Since the great majority of the Arab world is Muslim, many Lebanese Americans lacked a feeling of common background and interest with other Arab peoples.

This picture has changed dramatically in recent years. A bloody and destructive war has engulfed Lebanon in internal conflict, attack, and subversion by outside powers. Moreover, the nation has become entangled in complicated relationships with the Big Powers, including the United States. Two major changes affecting Lebanese Americans have resulted from this situation.

One is heightened awareness of the need to make public in the United States the "case" for Lebanon. New organizations have come into existence since 1975, and older ones have stepped up their activity. Some are concerned specifically with the plight of Lebanon and with the special interests of certain groups. One such is the American Lebanese League, based in Washington, D.C. This organization seeks to publicize issues affecting Lebanon, especially from the viewpoint of Maronite Christians, and to encourage among Lebanese Americans an interest in the "unique political-social-cultural character of Lebanon."

In the late 1970s, another organization, the Lebanon Information and Research Center, was opened in Washington representing a coalition of the major Christian political parties in Lebanon. Its mission is to encourage Christian Lebanese Americans to support the continuation of a dominant role

The bloody civil war in Lebanon has caused many Lebanese Americans to take a renewed interest in their ancestral homeland and the suffering of its inhabitants.

for Christian political groups in Lebanon.

Asserting the viewpoint of the Druze community is an organization called the American Druze Public Affairs Committee, established in 1983. Its aim is to inform American public officials and American citizens about the Druze involvement in the Lebanese struggle, thereby correcting some of the misunderstandings about this small but powerful minority.

Representing broader interests, a Washington-based organization called Save Lebanon, founded in 1981, has

been concerned specifically with medical help for victims of the fighting, especially children. At the University of Maryland, a newsletter called "Lebanon Monitor" has been issued since 1983. It focuses on constructive efforts toward ending the war and also on activities of Lebanese-American groups and their relations with the old country.

Other organizations treat the ongoing Lebanese crisis as part of the much larger need to publicize the Arab viewpoint. Probably the most prominent group of this nature is the American-Arab Anti-Discrimination Committee,

Former Senator James Abourezk, founder and national chairman of the American-Arab Anti-Discrimination Committee (ADC), testifies before a House committee on criminal justice.

established in 1980 with branches in cities coast to coast. Its primary aims are to combat the degrading images of Arabs in the media and public opinion and to fight discrimination against Arab Americans.

Founded in 1985, the Arab American Institute in Washington promotes political activism, encouraging Arab Americans to register to vote and to run for public office. The National Association of Arab Americans, started in 1972, seeks to combat the information gap between the United States and Arab countries and to promote ties of friendship, as well as to encourage political participation by Arab Americans.

Lebanese Americans, and Arab Americans in general, have long been without an effective voice to make known their views and needs on the political level. This has been due in part to lack of experience in public relations but also, unfortunately, to lack of interest and awareness. With the fate of Lebanon so uncertain, however, many Lebanese Americans now recognize the need to be better organized and more outspoken.

In 1986, concern for Lebanon's future prodded a Lebanese-American group to start a program that received national publicity. The Lebanese community of Fresno, California, joined forces with the Children's Committee 10, an organization that has been bringing children from troubled northern Ireland to the United States for summer visits. Thanks to generous donations, 16 teenagers from war-torn parts of

Lebanese-American groups have made special efforts to help children whose lives have been devastated by the fighting in Lebanon.

Lebanon were brought to spend six weeks with American families across the country. They were placed in pairs, in each case combining a Christian with a Muslim or Druze. These young people took back home new friendships with members of other religious groups—and a glimmering of hope for reconciliation in Lebanon.

Recent immigrants from Lebanon learn English in a Dearborn, Michigan, school.

New Immigrants from Lebanon

The second major result of the trouble in Lebanon has been yet another wave of emigration from the home country. Not surprisingly, large numbers of those people who have the money to leave and without compelling reasons for staying have departed the country. The United States is again the destination of many of these "refugee emigrants." The American government has eased restrictions on immigration from Lebanon, particularly for students and other individuals with family here.

These newcomers present a striking contrast with the early immigrants who arrived with nothing but their wits and willingness to work. The recent immigrants include many of the best educated people of Lebanon, with impressive professional qualifications and business experience. Often coming to join family members who emigrated earlier and are now well established and prosperous, they intend to continue their education, pursue their professions, or become involved in a good business (and not by starting at the bottom).

These latest immigrants have much in common with those who came from Lebanon in the 1950s and 1960s, but they differ from them in some important ways. The earlier immigrants, also well qualified in education and the professions, had strong feelings of Arab identity and a concern with Arab culture and the problems of the Middle East. By and large, recent immigrants, particularly Maronite Christians, do not share this outlook. The war in Lebanon has produced a hardening of political attitudes and stronger allegiance to the various religious groups.

Besides the educated emigrants, numbers of workers have also left Lebanon, having lost jobs and often homes due to warfare. In this group are many Shi'ite Muslims from south Lebanon, where war damage has been severe. In the United States, Detroit is the destination for most of these newcomers, and the sudden influx of immigrants in that area is a cause of social and political concern.

The people who have come to the United States in the last 10 years or so have been escaping from an intolerable situation or seeking a chance to do what they cannot do in Lebanon at this time. Many of them are the sort of people who can most benefit the United States —and who are, or will be, most needed in Lebanon. In their new lives, therefore, they face a difficult dilemma. Should they decide to make a permanent home in the United States? Or should they hope to return someday to Lebanon and help make it strong again?

The problem particularly affects Lebanese Christians. If too many Christians leave Lebanon, then those who remain may become a much weaker minority. There will be little chance to maintain the religious and cultural diversity that has characterized Lebanon for centuries. That diversity has been a source of both strength and strife, but, in either case, it has been what makes the country of Lebanon unique in the Middle East.

Many questions, agonizing ones, hover over the future of Lebanon. They affect the future of Lebanese Americans and their relations with the old country and the family members remaining there. Whatever happens, friends of Lebanon can only hope for solutions that will allow this 5,000-year-old country to continue its long history on a healthy basis.

9
THE LEBANESE IN AMERICA TOMMORROW

Two Detroit women in the 1920s wear the traditional costumes of their Lebanese ancestors.

The Lebanese experience in the United States has been an unusually happy one, almost completely free of the stresses that many other immigrant groups have had to face at one time or another. This is partly due to the small numbers of these immigrants and, perhaps more, to the character of both individuals and communities.

As we have seen, the emotional ties are still strong between Lebanese Americans and the old country. Those who remember Lebanon speak of its many beauties—and its delicious fruit. They long to go back to visit, as do their children and their grandchildren. But when asked if they would like Lebanon to be their final resting place, typically they answer with a firm "No." The United States has been good to them. It is "their country" now, they say, and it is where they want to remain.

Yet troubling questions are not far removed from even the most secure Lebanese-American family. One concerns the inevitable changes in Lebanon and the character that the country will assume in the coming years. These cannot be predicted with any certainty at the present time. Nor can the effect that developments in the Middle East may have upon Lebanese communities in the United States.

Another is the question of whether Lebanese Americans will want to emphasize their distinctiveness from other Arab peoples, as they have in the past. Or will they stress their unity with the Arab world, as increasing numbers do now. If they choose the second option, and especially if they become involved in political issues concerning the Middle East, then they may face the problems that other Arabs in the United States now encounter. Some of these problems come from outside the Arab-American community: insults and discrimination, denial of freedom of expression, even acts of violence. Other problems may arise from changes within the Arab community, particularly the growth of Islamic fundamentalism, which tends to isolate Muslim Arab groups from the surrounding American society.

Lebanese Americans also encounter the dilemmas faced by every other ethnic minority. How much of the old ways—food, religion, social customs, values—should be preserved? How "different" should Lebanese Americans be? Or should they aim at the ideal of

A recent Lebanese immigrant leads a demonstration in Dearborn supporting the Palestinian cause.

"homogenized American"? Who will preserve the old ways if young people lose interest or reject the customs of their parents and grandparents? Fortunately, after decades of covering over cultural differences and striving for "100-percent Americanism," Lebanese Americans, like other ethnic groups, are now proudly reviving interest in their heritage. It is doubtless too late for most young people today to learn Arabic in the home, since their parents and even grandparents neglected the native language. But national feeling now includes pride in the Lebanese and Arabic

Boys at a Dearborn street fair pose for their photograph against a background of factories and smokestacks. Young Americans like these are experiencing a renewed pride in their ethnic heritage.

culture as much as in the American. If variety is the spice of life, then American society can only be enriched by preservation of the distinctive Lebanese culture in the United States.

Among our most enthusiastically loyal citizens, Lebanese Americans have contributed much to both of the countries with which they have ties. They provide a solid foundation for good relations between the United States and Lebanon, which should become even stronger in the future.

INDEX

Dearborn, Michigan, Muslim community in, 28, 40

DeBakey, Lois, 66

DeBakey, Michael, 68-69

debki, 56

Detroit, Michigan, Muslim community in, 28, 40, 87

Dibs, Eddie, 75

Druze, 13, 15-16, 28, 54

education, Lebanese attitudes toward, 48, 66

Egypt, 21

Elias, Rosalind, 72

factory jobs, immigrants employed in, 38-39, 40

Fakhr-ed-Deen II, 11-12

family businesses, 37, 63

family life, importance of, 49-50, 57, 59, 62

Farah, Mansour, 39, 76

Farr, Jamie, 74

festivals, Lebanese, 55-56

Flutie, Doug, 75

food, Lebanese, 56

Fort Wayne, Indiana, peddling center in, 34

France, 11, 13; influence of, on Lebanon, 14

George, Bill, 75

Gibran, Kahlil (poet), 41, 42-43, 53, 62

Gibran, Kahlil (sculptor), 72

Gibran, Kamila, 62

Gibron, Abe, 75

Greek Catholics, 16

Greek influence in Lebanon, 8-9

Greek Orthodox Church, 16, 28, 50

Habib, Philip, 69

Haddad, Ameen, 76

Haggar, J. M., 76

Halaby, Najeeb, 69

Hitti, Philip, 71

Al-Hoda, 53

Islam, 9, 28, 52-53, 54

Islamic fundamentalism, 52, 89

Israel, 6, 14, 82

Kasem, Casey, 74

Kazen, Abraham, 70

Kfeir, 80

Khal, Helen, 67

Latimer, George, 70

Lebanese, use of name, 45-46

Lebanon Information and Research Center, 82-83

"Lebanon Monitor," 83

mahrajan, 56

Makassed, 28

Maloof, James, 70

Maloof, Sam, 77

Mandates, 13

Maronite Christians, 9, 11, 13, 14, 50, 83, 87;
   emigration of, to U.S., 27-28
   position of, in Lebanese society, 16-17

Melkite Christians, 16, 28, 50, 51

missionaries in Lebanon, 22, 26, 28

Mitchell, George, 70

Moffett, Toby, 70

mosques in U.S., 52

Mount Lebanon, 6, 13-14, 17, 18, 45;
   independence of, during 19th century, 11-13, 15, 19, 21

Muslims: in Lebanon, 9, 15; in U. S., 28, 40-41, 52-53

Nader, Laura, 66

Nader, Ralph, 70-71

Naff, Alixa, 67

names, Lebanese, 46

National Association of Arab Americans, 85

newspapers, 53

New York, Lebanese settlements in, 32

North Dakota, Lebanese settlement in, 33

Oakar, Mary Rose, 70

Oklahoma!, Arab peddler in, 34

Ottoman Empire, 11-13, 19-20, 24, 28, 45-46

Palestinians in Lebanon, 14

peddlers, Lebanese, 33-37; attitudes toward, 36; goods sold by, 36; networks of, 34; women as, 62-63

Pen League, 53

This Lebanese girl is taking part in a Maronite celebration of Palm Sunday held in Detroit, Michigan, during the 1920s.

ACKNOWLEDGMENTS The photographs in this book are reproduced through the courtesy of: pp. 2 (Florence Casseb), 38 (Malouf Abraham), 39 (Vivian Hertzog), 44 (Mrs. Bertha Davis), 94 (Harvey Fadal, Sr.), Institute of Texan Cultures at San Antonio; pp. 6, 7, 12, 15, 19, 20, Independent Picture Service; pp. 9, 10, 16, 25, 83 (right), 96, Lebanese Information & Research Center; p. 17, Israel Museum; pp. 18, 71 (bottom), Hitti Collection, Immigration History Research Center, University of Minnesota; pp. 22, 45, National Park Service, Statue of Liberty National Monument; pp. 23, 26, 80, American University of Beirut; p. 27, *Frank Leslie's Illustrated Historical Register of the Centennial Exposition, 1876*; pp. 29, 40, 52, 57, 86, 89, 90, Millard Berry; pp. 30, 31, 78, Utah State Historical Society; pp. 32, 42, Library of Congress; pp. 34, 74 (top left and right), Collectors Bookstore; pp. 35, 37, 55, 56, 58, 88, 93, Warren W. David; pp. 43, 62, Jean and Kahlil Gibran (from *Kahlil Gibran,* New York Graphic Society, 1974); pp. 47, 60, 61, 65, Angela Azar; pp. 48-49, Stanley Rashid; p. 50, St. Maron Catholic Church, Minneapolis, Minnesota; p. 51, *Worcester Telegram & Gazette, Inc.*; p. 54, Joan Z. Farrier; pp. 59, 79, Bernice T. Scully; p. 64, Zarefa Ray; pp. 66, 68, Baylor College of Medicine; p. 67, Salwa Showker Roosevelt; p. 69 (top), Philip Habib; p. 69 (bottom), Congressman Nick Rahall; p. 70 (top), Governor Victor Atiyeh; p. 70 (bottom), Mayor George Latimer; p. 71 (top), Wide World Photos; p. 72, Metropolitan Opera; p. 73 (top), Kahlil Gibran; p. 73 (bottom), St. Jude Children's Research Hospital; p. 74 (bottom), Casey Kasem, American Top 40; p. 75 (left), Chicago Bears; p. 75 (right), New Jersey Generals; p. 76, Haggar Apparel Company; p. 77, Sam Maloof, photo by Schenck & Schenck; p. 81, Mary Mokarzel Collection, Immigration History Research Center, University of Minnesota; p. 83 (left), 85, United Nations; p. 84, Nancy Shia, photo courtesy of American-Arab Anti-Discrimination Committee. Front cover photograph: Malouf Abraham, courtesy of Institute of Texan Cultures. Back cover photographs: Mrs. Bertha Davis, courtesy of Institute of Texan Cultures (upper left); Collectors Bookstore (lower left); Utah State Historical Society (right).

The Fadal drugstore in Waco, Texas, during the 1930s

ELSA MARSTON HARIK has long had a deep interest in the countries and cultures of the Middle East, particularly in Lebanon. After receiving a master's degree in international affairs at Radcliffe College, she continued her graduate studies at the American University of Beirut, and it was here that she met her future husband, Iliya Harik, a native of Lebanon. Following their marriage, the Hariks lived in Lebanon, Egypt, and Tunisia, while Dr. Harik, a political scientist, did research and his wife devoted herself to painting and writing. Her novels for young readers, written under the name of Elsa Marston, are set in the Middle Eastern locales that she knows so well. Ms Marston's published works also include articles, short stories, and a young people's book on American archaeology mysteries. Today Elsa Marston Harik lives in Bloomington, Indiana, where her husband teaches comparative politics at Indiana University. The Hariks have three sons, one of whom was born in Lebanon. Mrs. Harik last visited Lebanon in 1975, and since then, she has kept in close touch with the country through relatives and friends.

THE IN AMERICA SERIES

Lerner Publications Company
241 First Avenue North · Minneapolis, Minnesota 55401